CONFECTIONERY IN YORKSHIRE
THROUGH TIME
Paul Chrystal

AMBERLEY PUBLISHING

Creme tangerine and Montelimar, A ginger sling with a pineapple heart, A coffee desert – yes you know it's good news ... cool cherry crème and a nice apple tart ... coconut fudge really blows down those blues.
George Harrison (1943–2001), Savoy Truffle

Acknowledgements

Thanks to the following for their generosity and patience in providing images and information, without their kindness this book could not have been published: Alex Hutchinson, Nestlé Heritage, York; Dr Amanda Jones and colleagues, Borthwick Institute, University of York; Sarah Brown, Brand Manager and Tony Wade, Tangerine Confectionery; Robert Cunningham-Brown, Caley of Norwich Ltd; Sarah Foden, Kraft Foods for the images of and information on Maynard's and Bassett's; Sarah McKee, Bettys & Taylors of Harrogate; Beth Hurrell, Joseph Rowntree Foundation; Miriam and Stephen Walshaw, Joseph Dobson & Sons Ltd; Sarah Oselton, Haribo UK; Wendy Jewitt and Dawn Bartram, Library Development Area Supervisors, Wakefield Council; Leanne Dodds, Registrar and Collections Officer, Wakefield Council; Claire Simpson, William Jackson Food Group; Andrew Littlewood for the information and pictures on Thorne's of Leeds and some of the more obscure Yorkshire confectioners; Sophie Jewett, Director, York Cocoa House and Little Pretty Things, York; Raymond Needler for permission to use images and information originally published in his definitive *Needlers of Hull*; William and John Whitaker, Whitakers Chocolates Ltd; Monk Bar Chocolatiers, York.

About the Author

Paul Chrystal is author of the following titles in the Amberley Publishing *Through Time* series: *Knaresborough*; *North York Moors*; *Tadcaster*; *Villages Around York*; *Richmond & Swaledale*; *Northallerton*; *Hartlepool*; *In & Around York*; *Harrogate*; *York Places of Learning*; *Redcar, Marske & Saltburn*; *Vale of York*; *In & Around Pocklington*; *Barnard Castle & Teesdale*; *Lifeboat Stations of the North East*, 2012.

Other books by Paul Chrystal: *A Children's History of Harrogate & Knaresborough*; *A to Z of Knaresborough History Revised Ed*; *A to Z of York History*, 2012; *Women in Rome*, 2013.

His confectionery related books include *Chocolate: The British Chocolate Industry*, Shire 2011; *The History of Chocolate in York*, Pen & Sword 2012; *The Rowntree Family & York*, Amberley 2012; *Fry & Cadbury Through Time*, Amberley 2012; *Tea, Coffee & Cocoa Through Time*, Amberley 2012; *Model Industrial Towns & Villages Through Time*, Amberley 2012.

As well as being author and historian, Paul was a medical publisher for thirty years and, more recently, a bookseller; he lives near York.

First published 2012

Amberley Publishing
The Hill, Stroud
Gloucestershire, GL5 4EP

www.amberley-books.com

Copyright © Paul Chrystal, 2012

The right of Paul Chrystal to be identified as the Author of this work has been asserted in accordance with the Copyrights, Designs and Patents Act 1988.

ISBN 978 1 4456 0909 6

British Library Cataloguing in Publication Data.
A catalogue record for this book is available from the British Library.

Typeset in 9.5pt on 12pt Celeste.
Typesetting by Amberley Publishing.
Printed in the UK.

Introduction

Yorkshire has been home to more confectionery companies over the years than any other region of Britain – and it's by no means just Rowntree's, Terry's and Mackintosh; there is a lot more to it than just York or Halifax. Needler's of Hull, Thornton's and Bassett's of Sheffield and Thorne's of Leeds have all been significant forces in the industry – the two Sheffield companies still are. Indeed, Whitaker's of Skipton, Dobson's of Elland, Riley of Halifax and Simpkin in Sheffield have nineteenth- or early twentieth-century origins and, along with Lion Confectionery in Cleckheaton, are still trading successfully today, the first three with retail outlets. Add to this the liquorice companies around Pontefract, Doncaster, the home of butterscotch, and land-locked Dewsbury where Slade & Bullock perfected seaside rock, and there is clearly much to take into account in any history of confectionery in Yorkshire.

This book is the first to be published which traces that history in pictures and in words from the early beginnings in the eighteenth and nineteenth centuries. Making use of packaging – showcards, tins, wrappers – advertisements and old archive photographs juxtaposed with new equivalents, it graphically traces the development of the industry down the years to the present day. And it's not just huge international conglomerates that prevail, as companies like Dobson's, Whitaker's, Tangerine and Simpkin's so obviously prove.

Nearly 200 images supported by an informative text will delight and inform anyone interested in industrial, social, food and marketing history. Anyone who worked, or still works, in any of the twenty-five or so confectionery companies covered here will enjoy a nostalgic journey through the past that takes them from Hull to Leeds and Elland, from Sheffield to York and Skipton, with many points in between.

The book concludes with a look at the industry in Yorkshire today, where it seems we are just waking up to the realisation that this is the confectionery capital of the United Kingdom. A plethora of independent chocolatiers and cocoa houses are springing up on many high streets and the county at long last has an archive at Nestlé in York, a new visitor centre in the fascinating Sweet History of York, and the first York Chocolate Festival – all to celebrate Yorkshire's marvellous confectionery heritage.

Paul Chrystal, York, 2012

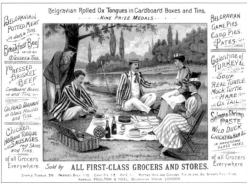

The first picture shows very clearly that the appeal of the sweet shop to children has endured down the years; compare the photograph on page 21. The second shows cocoa harvesting in the West Indies. The third depicts a well-to-do picnic provisioned by an equally well-to-do London grocer – it shows what confectionery was up against in the middle class consumer market. The 1915 poster for Banania has had its share of controversy for its depiction of the Senegalese Tirailleur as an exploited victim of colonialism; it promotes this cocoa based drink, still available today. The 1902 Bovril poster is illustrated by John Hassall; Bovril Chocolate could boast 300 per cent more nourishment than regular chocolate. Van Houten's reminds us of the competition from abroad and from other products.

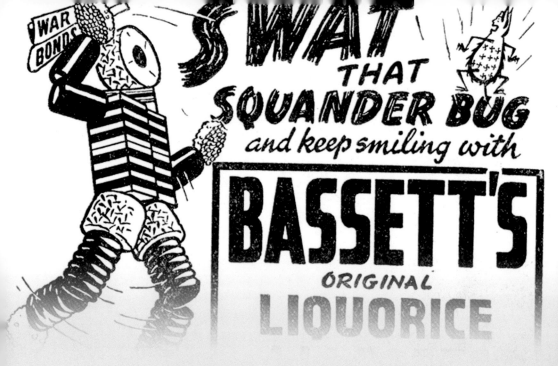

CHAPTER 1

Bassett's, Sheffield

CONFECTIONARY WORKS.

PORTLAND ST INFIRMARY ROAD, SHEFFIELD.
BASSETT & LODGE, PROPRIETORS.

BASSETT & LODGE,
MANUFACTURERS OF ALL KINDS OF
GENUINE LOZENGES,
Fancy and Medicated; Plain or Stamped with the Retailer's name as a
GUARANTEE OF THEIR PURITY.

B. & L. have fitted up two "PATENT CONFECTION PANS," for the Manufacture
of all kinds of
COMFITS,
THE ONLY PANS OF THE KIND IN ENGLAND.

Great attention is paid to the
SUGAR BOILING DEPARTMENT,
No Colour being used that is in the slightest degree Injurious.

PATE DE JU-JUBES AND PASTILLES DE GOMME
Are prepared in their Steam Pans and Cut up by Machinery.

B. & L. likewise Manufacture
JUICE, LIQUORICE PIPES, AND PONTEFRACT CAKES.

Being importers of LEMONS they can supply
CANDIED LEMON,
Equal to any House in the Trade.

MANUFACTURERS OF
REAL SCOTCH MARMALADE.

AGENTS FOR HUNTLEY AND PALMER'S READING BISCUITS,
AND
NELSON'S GELATINE LOZENGES.

EXPORT HOUSES Supplied on the most ADVANTAGEOUS TERMS.

R. KING, ENGRAVER AND PRINTER, SHEFFIELD.

...British Wine Dealer

Founded in 1842 by George Bassett, Sheffield, 'wholesale confectioner, lozenge maker and British wine dealer', the company opened its first factory in Portland Street in 1852 before moving to larger premises in Owlerton around 1900. Bassett's partner was Samuel Meggitt Johnson (his future son-in-law) and they employed around 200 workers in what was the world's biggest sweet manufactory at the time. The Sheffield factory is today Cadbury's centre for sugar confectionery in the UK. Bassett's three most important brands are: Liquorice Allsorts, Jelly Babies, and Wine Gums. The older image on page 5 shows a Second World War advertisement warning about zoning; the new photograph shows Bassett's today. Page 6 depicts the first factory and a sales 'catalogue' from around the same time.

Unclaimed Babies

Geo. Bassett & Co Ltd bought Wilkinsons of Pontefract, famous for their Pontefract cakes, Barratt's in 1966 (sherbet fountains and sweet cigarettes) and Trebor (the eponymous mints) before being bought themselves by Cadbury's in 1989. Jelly Babies were originally conceived by an Austrian confectioner working for Fryers of Lancashire in the 1860s and branded as Unclaimed Babies. Bassett's Jelly Babies were launched in 1918 to celebrate the end of the First World War; then they were called Peace Babies. Production was halted during the Second World War, resuming in 1953 when rationing finally ended; they then became known as Jelly Babies. The Beatles were often pelted with them and successive Doctor Whos have used them as a negotiating tool to take the steam out of tense situations. Screaming Jelly Babies are the dramatic result of a school experiment when the sweets are immersed in a strong oxidising agent.

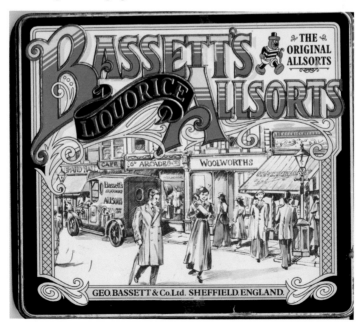

Bertie Bassett

The origin of Liquorice Allsorts is legendary. In 1899, Charlie Thompson, a sales representative, was on a call in Leicester when he dropped a tray of samples all over the floor. These had already been rejected as individual purchases but the resulting colourful, random mix so impressed the shopkeeper that he placed an order for what was soon to become the Allsorts. Bertie Bassett is the Bassett company mascot, a man made entirely from liquorice allsorts created by John (Jack) McEwan and introduced to the sweet-buying public on 1 January 1929. He was obviously inspired by the highly successful Michelin Man. Today, the allsorts mix contains a son of Bertie: a diminutive aniseed and liquorice figure in Bertie's image.

Our favourite.

Which sort of Allsort is your sort?

Bassett's
Liquorice Allsorts

Betty Bassett

The *Doctor Who* serial *The Happiness Patrol* featured the evil Kandy Man, who bore an uncanny likeness to Bertie Bassett. Bertie, however, triumphed: an out-of-court settlement led to oblivion for Kandy Man, sentenced to eternal exile. To celebrate his eightieth birthday in 2009, Bertie married his 'sweetheart' Betty Bassett (no relation we hope) in the Sheffield factory with workers enjoying the ceremony as guests included even a best man.

Liquorice-Free Allsorts

By 1966 they were the largest sugar confectionery manufacturers in Britain employing 1,300 people. Bassett's now also produce liquorice-free varieties of allsorts devoid of all liquorice: Fruit Allsorts feature mixed-fruit flavours; Dessert Allsorts include apple tart and lemon cheesecake. There is also a red liquorice Betty Bassett. Zoning, as in the Second World War advertisement, was the practice where transportation of goods was limited, companies' sales territories were limited and companies had to take on the manufacture of goods of companies outside the zone.

CHAPTER 2

Betty & Taylors, Harrogate

A FULL SCALE A.R.P. TEST. the first of its kind, took place in Harrogate on Sunday.

Eat Chocolate and Lose Weight

The story of Bettys began in September 1907 when a twenty-two-year-old Fritz Butzer arrived in England from Switzerland with no English and less of any idea of how to reach a town that sounded vaguely like 'Bratwurst', where a job awaited him. Fritz eventually landed up in Bradford and found work with a Swiss confectioner called Bonnet & Sons at 44 Darley Street. Cashing in on the vogue for all things French, Fritz changed his name to Frederick Belmont; he opened his first business in July 1919 – a café in Cambridge Crescent, Harrogate, on three floors fitted out to the highest standards. The Bettys advertisement tell us that sound German medical research proves that eating chocolate leads to weight loss and is beneficial in the fight against heart disease. Bettys team of eight chocolatiers have over 135 years experience of hand-crafting chocolates between them. See page 96.

"Here is your *Fortune* my pretty maid!"

CHAPTER 3

Caley, Norwich & Halifax

Mineral Waters, Crackers and Chocolate

Caley was originally a manufacturer of mineral waters founded in 1863; their entry into the confectionery market was a strategic move to balance out the seasonal water market. In 1857 Albert Jarman Caley opened a chemist's business in London Street, Norwich; in 1883 he started manufacturing drinking chocolate as a winter drink to balance out the year followed by eating chocolate in 1886, made at the Fleur-de-Lys factory. In 1898 Christmas cracker manufacture began, to keep the girls who wrapped and decorated the chocolate boxes busy all year round; A. J. Caley & Sons Ltd was formed at this time. In 1918 the African and Eastern Trade Corporation bought Caley – a Liverpool company with interests in a number of African colonies; it later became a Unilever subsidiary.

Double Six Sandwiches

In 1932 John Mackintosh & Sons Ltd of Halifax paid £138,000 for Caley, although the Caley's brand name continued to be used until the early 1960s. In 1935 mineral water production dried up; in 1936 Double Six was successfully launched – a chocolate bar filled with six different centres. The public's response was described by Eric Mackintosh as 'a little frightening'. Miners' wives in South Wales were giving their husbands Double Six sandwiches in their pack-ups. The wonderful Caley advertisements and posters are depicted here, some of which were drawn by Sir Alfred Mullins. The Easter egg box was illustrated by John Hassall and features Ruff-and-Ready, protagonist in May Byron's *The Magic Shop*, 1905.

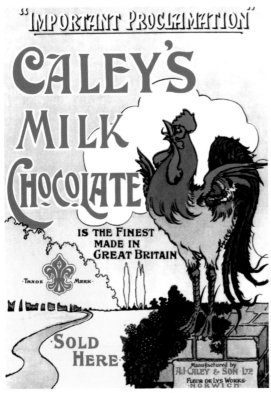

The Baedecker Raid

The Second World War saw the first production of sustaining 'cocoa rich' Milk Marching Chocolate. In 1942 Caley's factory was destroyed by the Luftwaffe in the Baedecker Raid (see page 13); Eric Mackintosh described the scene: 'a smouldering, smelling, twisted jumble of steel and concrete … [watched] by a crowd of tired, dirty, heart-broken colleagues … a thousand or so employees stood around, dazed and unable to believe their eyes'. The factory re-opened after rebuilding work in 1956; production of Caley lines had been moved to Halifax in the interim. Mackintosh merged with Rowntree in 1969 to form Rowntree Mackintosh. Norwich took on production of Weekend, Good News, Rolo, Munchies, Mintola, Caramac, Golden Cup and Easter eggs, and, paradoxically, Yorkie. The Norwich factory closed in 1994; in 1996 three former executives acquired Caley's brands and production equipment from Nestlé and formed Caley's of Norwich Ltd. In 1997 Caley's Plain Marching Chocolate was relaunched and in 1998 Caley's Milk Marching Chocolate was reintroduced. The cockerel showcard dates from around 1905; the fashionable coy lady from the 1920s.

CHAPTER 4

Craven, York

Hick, Hide and Craven

Craven's dates back to 1803 when Joseph Hick, aged twenty-nine, set up in York as Kilner & Hick, confectioners. Kilner left the business to Hick which he relocated to 47 Coney Street, next door to what was then the Leopard Inn and opposite St Martin's Church. Mary Ann was born in 1829, Hick's youngest daughter. In 1833 Thomas Craven, son of an East Acklam farmer, arrived in York aged sixteen as apprentice to Thomas Hide, his brother-in-law. Hide was running a confectionery business established in the mid to late 1820s called George Berry & Thomas Hide after the joint owners and located at 20 High Ousegate. Thomas Craven bought the right to trade in York when he became a Freeman in 1840; on Hide's death in 1843 he set up his own business next door at 19 High Ousegate. The gentlemen pictured are celebrating their long service records in 1913 stretching from forty-five to sixty-five years. Mary Ann Craven features in the other picture. The production shot on page 17 shows workers in the 1970s making golden humbugs.

York's First Confectionery Museum

On 1 May 1845 Craven moved the business to 31 Pavement, not far from the Rowntree's shop and in 1851 he married Mary Ann Hick – she was twenty-two, he thirty-four. In 1860 Joseph Hick died; then in 1862 Mary Ann's husband died leaving her with three young children (one boy and two girls aged eight, six and four) to raise and two businesses to run. She was equal to the challenge: she amalgamated the two businesses, changed the name of the company to MA Craven, and ran it until 1902 (page 18). Production was now in Coppergate (page 17) – roughly where the Jorvik Viking Centre is now – along with additional properties in Coney Street and Foss Islands Road. Staff numbers had increased to 800 by 1908 – a sizeable business by York standards. There were four Craven's retail shops in the city one of which, Craven's Mary Ann Sweet Shop, was in the Shambles and featured a sweet museum on the first floor where visitors could see 150 years of the 'Art, Trade, Mystery and Business of the Confectioner'. The pictures show Craven jars and wrappers on display in 2012, many of which were recently found quite by chance when a warehouse was being cleared.

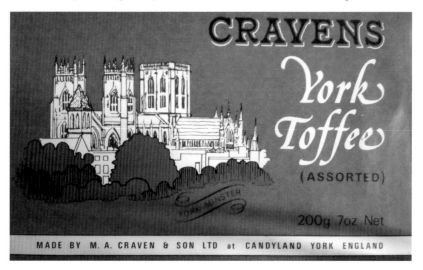

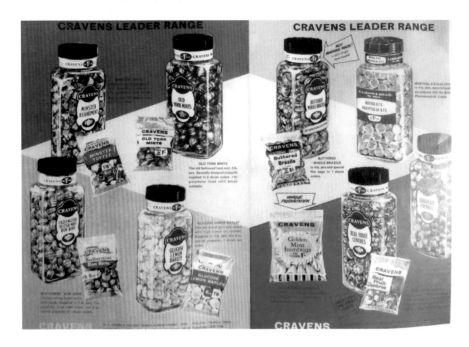

Monkhill, Sir Kreemy Knut and Tangerine

In 1920 the Coppergate factory was named The French Almond Works in recognition of the importance of that product line. In 1992 Craven's bought Crusader, Barker & Dobson, Keillers & Bensons and Milady; the company was subsequently renamed Craven Keiller in 1995. Trebor Bassett bought Craven in 1996 and in 1999 the York and Pontefract factories combined to form Monkhill Confectionery, later owned by Cadbury Schweppes. In 2004 Monkhill re-launched the entire Sharps of York range with the monocled cartoon aristocrat named Sir Kreemy Knut who had featured in Sharp's marketing at launch in 1911. In February 2008 Tangerine Confectionery bought Monkhill from Cadbury Schweppes for £58 million.

CHAPTER 5

J. Dobson & Sons, Elland

Funeral Biscuits
One of the largest privately owned
confectionery manufacturers in Yorkshire.
Joseph Dobson came to Elland in 1850
with his young bride, Eleanor, from York.
The twenty-one-year-old Joseph had come
to collect his inheritance, only to find
that his solicitor had absconded with it.
Notwithstanding, Joseph and Eleanor set
up business, catering mainly for Victorian
family occasions producing wedding cakes
and funeral biscuits.

This is the Original Wrapper of
Joseph Dobson, founder of the Firm of
Joseph Dobson & Sons, Limited.
Date of Printing, 1852.

FROM

J. DOBSON,
GENERAL CONFECTIONER,
Northgate,
ELLAND.

Bride Cakes and Funeral Biscuits and all
kinds of Confectionery to order on the
shortest notice, and on the most
reasonable terms.

Voice Confectionery

By the time he was ten, both Joseph's parents had died from plague and he was raised by his grandparents. As a boy he worked for Cravens in York. Eleanor was the sister of William Charles Berry, confectioner and Freeman of the city of York. The Berry's were joint founders of Terry's. Many early sweets claimed some medicinal benefit; indeed early pharmaceuticals sweetened with sugar or honey coatings were called electuaries, or confections. Confectionery soon became another word for sweets as the medicinal element receded. Dobson's still produce Voice Tablets to this day – efficacious against sore throats. C. T. & W. Holloway, Birmingham confectioners, made Voice Confectionery. In 1895 Holloway somehow obtained the endorsement of the famous Spanish soprano Adelina Patti; they eponymously rebranded their lozenges Pattines, put her likeness on the tin and added the pithy Patti endorsement: 'much pleased'. The pictures show displays of Dobson's sweets today in their Elland shop (page 21).

'Take Ye Not To Strong Drink'

In the very early 1900s Joseph Dobson's introduced Conversation Lozenges, some of which promoted sound Victorian values such as 'Take Ye Not To Strong Drink' and 'Honour Your Parents'. London sweet maker F. Allen's followed a similar line in their cocoa advertisements: they depict contrasting domestic scenes where the cocoa drinkers are paragons of temperance and prosperity while their less abstemious neighbours are drowning in intemperance and poverty. George Cadbury and Joseph Rowntree would surely have endorsed these sentiments. The Conversation Lozenges were the precursors of the famous Love Hearts which Joseph Terry was making about the same time with such risqué messages as 'Can you polka?', 'I want a wife', 'Do you love me?' and 'How do you flirt?' Mint humbug making in the Northgate factory is shown in the old picture.

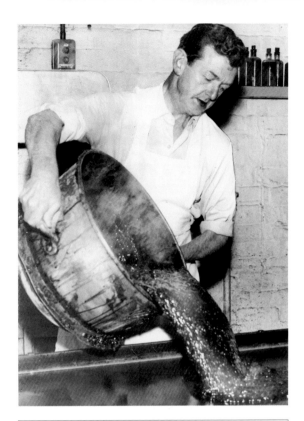

The Sweetie Man

The company has always been owned and managed by direct descendants of Joseph. Joseph, who died in 1885 at the age of fifty-six, left three sons, Robert Henry, William Charles and Thomas John, each of whom ran the company at one time or another. Dobson's have always enjoyed a reputation as *the* local 'sweetie man', ever active in local events, carnival processions, and mounting displays centred around the giant antique glass jars in shops, supermarkets and museums.

DOBSON'S OF ELLAND

PRESENT

4 ATTRACTIVE CHRISTMAS LINES.

1. BROWN HUMBUGS

a good quality Mint sweet made with brown sugar

2. WHITE HUMBUGS

the only difference is in the sugar — we use white for this.

They are EFFECTIVE against Indigestion

DOBSON'S BOILED SWEETS EST. 1850.

GUARANTEED PURE 2 LBS. NETT

BROWN HUMBUGS

2 lb. Tins 2/-
1 lb. Tins 1/-

— NETT WEIGHT —

BOILED SWEETS

25

Bonfire Toffee

The famous Yorkshire Mixtures were, like Liquorice Allsorts, named entirely by accident. One day Joseph's son, Thomas John, was carrying some sweets downstairs when he slipped and the eighteen varieties of sweets cascaded down the stairs. The resulting jumbled mixture was named Yorkshire Mixtures. Other vintage brands which have stood the test of time include Butter Mintoes made with real butter and flavoured with natural oil of peppermint; Menthol Mixtures, an assortment of four strong menthol and eucalyptus sweets; and Bonfire Toffee, a crispy toffee made with lots of black treacle and real butter.

CHAPTER 6

Dunhill & Other
Pontefract Manufacturers

Pomfrets

The area around Pontefract is famous for its cultivation of liquorice, a plant brought to the area from the Mediterranean by Dominican monks who settled here in the early sixteenth century. It was Sir George Saville who invented the Pontefract cake, or pomfret, in 1614 when he stamped the small, round liquorice cakes. Then they were eaten for medicinal purposes and it was only in 1760 when George Dunhill, an apothecary, added sugar to the cakes, thus transforming a medicinal confection into a sweet. Dunhill still operates from Pontefract and is owned by Haribo. Haribo was founded in 1920 by Hans Riegel Sr in Bonn, the name is an acronym for *Ha*ns *Ri*egel, *Bo*nn. Until the 1960s Pontefract cakes were handmade and hand stamped; an experienced stamper could turn out 30,000 cakes a day. The rug was made in 2006 and shows the companies associated with liquorice making in Pontefract; it was designed by Diane West and Margaret Kenny and made by members of the West Riding Ruggers (the black is made from women's tights) for the annual Liquorice Fair. Willie Wilko (Wilkinsons) is on the left with two Bertie Bassetts at the bottom. The Little Lord Fauntleroy figure is a Hillaby's figure; the castle is the logo of Sampson & Gundill.

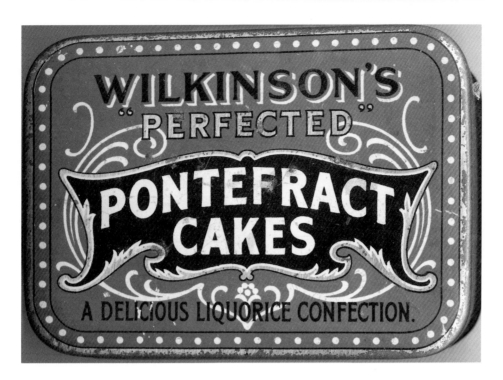

Wilkinson's and Willie Wilko

W. R. Wilkinson opened his first liquorice business in 1884 in a malt kiln in Southgate; soon after he moved to a new factory in Skinner Lane, the Britannia Works. In 1894 they moved again, to a former brush factory in Monkhill which was rebuilt in 1925 as a garden factory with tennis courts, allotments, and housing for some of the workers in the grounds. Willie Wilko (Willie Wilko says try my mints!) was born in 1946: if you saved fifteen packet tops you qualified for a Willie Wilko bendy toy. In 1900 Wilkinson's and Dunhill were two of eleven firms manufacturing liquorice in Pontefract; Wilkinson's are now owned by Tangerine Confectionery of York, having been bought by Bassett's in 1961.

29

Perfect
Harmony
and Blending

As specialists in the
production of high quality Liquorice
Confectionery, we can thoroughly
recommend these fast selling lines for
your counter. Packed in colourful display cartons.
you can depend on Ewbanks Liquorice
Allsorts, Pomfret Cakes and 1d. Novelties.

Ewbanks

EWBANKS LTD · EAGLE WORKS · PONTEFRACT · ENGLAND

Eubank's and Hillaby's
Eubank's was founded in 1810 by Thomas Firth; they operated from the Eagle Works and were named after Robert Eubank, a later owner. Liquorice as we know it is made by macerating liquorice roots and supplementing the juice with dried liquorice juice from Spain; this is the derivation of the Yorkshire dialect for liquorice, *Spanish*. A team of forty-five skilled women workers could press up to 25,000 Pontefract cakes per day. Hillaby's established their liquorice factory, the Lion Works, in 1850; they grew their own liquorice and by 1893 were the world's largest producer. They were taken over by Bellamy's of Castleford in 1943. Other local manufacturers included R. Austerbery & Co founded in 1888 at the Castle Moat Liquorice Refinery. Sampson & Gundill was established in 1889 at the Tower Liquorice Refinery and Robinson & Wordsworth from 1877 at the Victoria Works.

CHAPTER 7

Farrah's, Harrogate

Famous ..
for over
70 years.

Patronised
by H.M.
Queen Mary

Life's sweetest hours
are spent with

FARRAH'S
HARROGATE
TOFFEE

Palm Court Café Fine Chocolate Shop
John Farrah founded the business in 1840;
his shop was originally on Royal Parade but
closed in the mid-1990s and now stands on
Montpellier Parade as the Palm Court Café Fine
Chocolate Shop, pictured here. The purpose
of Farrah's Original Harrogate Toffee was
to cleanse the palate of the putrid taste of
Harrogate's sulphur water. Original Harrogate
Toffee is similar to both butterscotch and barley
sugar and uses three different types of sugar,
butter and lemon to give a unique texture and
flavour. It is still made in copper pans and
packaged in the recognisable trade mark blue
and silver embossed tins. The showcard dates
from around 1915.

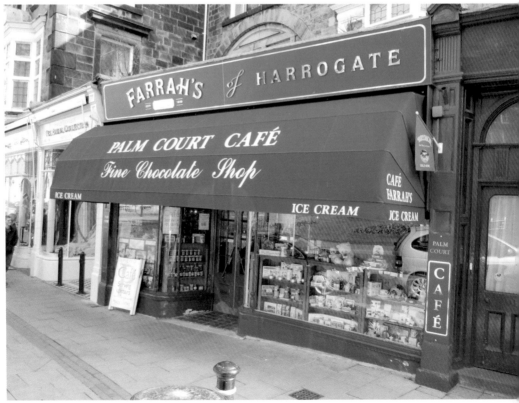

CHAPTER 8

Wm Jackson, Hull

Mr & Mrs Split Currant

William Jackson opened his first shop at 28 Scale Lane in September 1851 on the afternoon of his wedding. Parsimony, or value for money, has been an abiding principle: the Jacksons were known locally as Mr & Mrs Split Currant. Under William's son, George, the firm moved to 127 Spring Bank. By 1912 there were seventeen shops, a bakery in Derringham Street, a jam factory, warehousing and stables. By 1916 there were thirteen stores rising to eight-five in 1939. Today Wm Jackson Food Group owns a number of companies including Jackson's Bakery on the Derringham Street site. On page 33 the shop is the Hessle Square branch opened in 1927 and decked out for the George VI's coronation in May 1937, with shop manager Mr Allington in the dark coat. The vans were at Jackson's Stockton bakery in 1955. The photograph on this page shows driver John Holmes with his horse-drawn van in 1912. The other picture is of a tin from RK Confectionery, another Hull firm, exploiting the popularity of Felix the Cat films which were very popular around 1920.

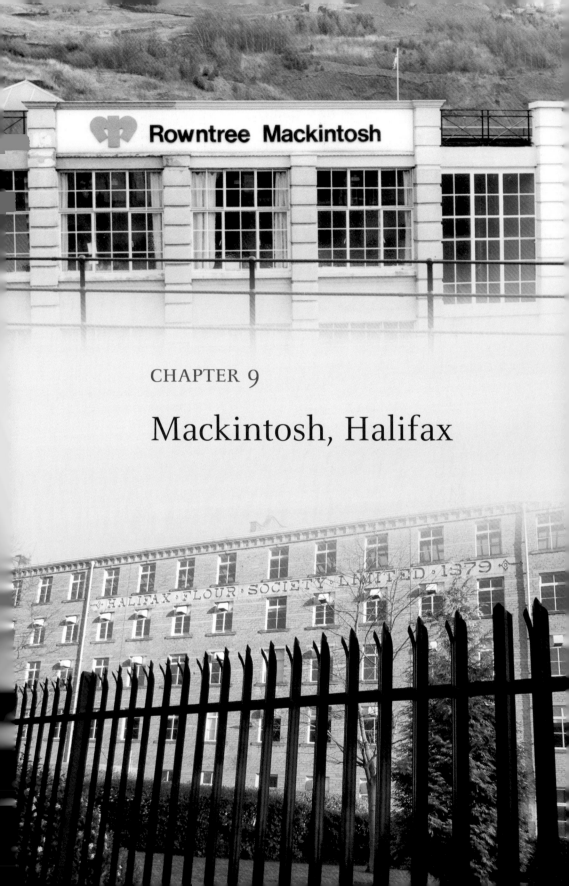

CHAPTER 9

Mackintosh, Halifax

'Toffee King'

John and Violet Mackintosh set up their business in a pastry shop in King Cross Lane in 1890 financing the company with the £100 they had saved between them. Their first launch was Mackintosh's Celebrated Toffee, a winning mixture of English butterscotch and American caramel. Mackintosh was nothing if not innovative – he exploited sampling to the full: one week he was inviting customers to come and taste a sample for free, the next he was urging them to come again and 'eat it at your expense'. Modest too: by 1896 Mackintosh was styling himself 'Toffee King'. The photographs on page 35 show the factory soon after the merger with Rowntree and part of it today in 2012. A magnificent 1921 Heath Robinson advertisement published in *Punch* is on this page; the line at the bottom boasts: 'in every Town and Village in the Kingdom ... obtainable in every country in the World'. The more modest Quality Street advert is from 1955.

'I am John Mackintosh, the Toffee King, Sovereign of Pleasure, Emperor of Joy'
Mackintosh was keen to develop his export trade, but this was not without its problems: in mainland Europe potential customers confused toffee with coffee and poured boiling water on it 'with unsatisfactory results'. In the US the extreme variations in climate wreaked havoc and, depending on the time of year, toffee was melting in some states and was rock hard in others. Notwithstanding, this is how he modestly heralded his entry into the US market: 'I am John Mackintosh, the Toffee King, Sovereign of Pleasure, Emperor of Joy. My old English candy tickles my millions of subjects...I was crowned by the lovers of good things to eat...I am the world's largest consumer of butter, my own herd of prize cattle graze on the Yorkshire hills. I buy sugar by the trainload. I am John Mackintosh, Toffee King of England and I rule alone.' His eloquence and industry were rewarded with ample success, even in intractable markets like China where the toffee he supplied was pink. The Dessert Chocolate advertisement was aimed squarely at men: it was published in a 1923 edition of *The Wide World: The Magazine for Men*.

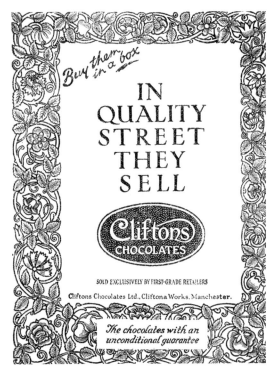

THE

W. H. SMITH & SON

AMATEUR

DRAMATIC SOCIETY

presents

Quality Street

at the

CRIPPLEGATE THEATRE
GOLDEN LANE, E.C.1

on

WEDNESDAY, THURSDAY and FRIDAY

June 1, 2 and 3

Buy them in a box

IN
QUALITY
STREET
THEY
SELL

Cliftons
CHOCOLATES

SOLD EXCLUSIVELY BY FIRST-GRADE RETAILERS

Cliftons Chocolates Ltd., Cliftona Works, Manchester.

*The chocolates with an
unconditional guarantee*

A. J. Caley of Norwich

In 1927 chocolate coated Toffee Deluxe was launched followed by Mackintosh Chocolate in 1924. John's son, Harold Mackintosh, later 1st Viscount Mackintosh of Halifax, took over in 1920. He developed the Methodist principles on which the firm had been founded, notably enlightened management and good labour relations. In 1932 he bought the A. J. Caley Norwich confectionery company from Unilever; this expanded their range of products and led to the launch of blockbuster products such as Quality Street in 1936 and Rolo in 1938. The images are of a programme for Quality Street signed by the cast and a Cliftons Chocolate advertisement showing that Mackintosh did not always have it all their own way in Quality Street.

The little Cherub Whispers

"There's a smile in every piece"

Mackintosh's Toffee de Luxe

You can also get the "Smiles" chocolate-coated.
Ask for Mackintosh's CHOCOLATE Toffee-de-Luxe.

MADE BY JOHN MACKINTOSH & SONS LTD HALIFAX

'Tis the Most Momentous Thing that has yet Happened in the World of Sweetness'

The Quality Street name was inspired by the play by *Peter Pan* author J. M. Barrie. 'Major Quality' and 'Miss Sweetly' owe their lives to the play's protagonists and appeared on all Quality Street packaging and advertising until 2000. They in turn were originally modelled by Iris and Tony Coles, the children of Sydney Coles who created the brand's image. Mackintosh took an advertisement on the front page of the *Daily Mail*, on 2 May 1936: 'An introduction to Quality Street'. It shows Miss Sweetly tempting Major Quality with a tin of the sweets. 'Sweets to the sweet, Miss Sweetly?' asks the Major, to which she coyly replies: 'Spare my blushes Major Quality, feast your eyes rather on this sumptuous array of toffees and chocolates ... 'tis the most momentous thing that has yet happened in the world of sweetness.' She gives him a 'toffee creme brazil' which he declares 'a veritable triumph!' The founder's blue plaque and the magnificent chimney at what is now the Nestlé plant are shown in the pictures.

The Purple One

Some seven million Quality Street chocolates are now produced every day, the most popular out of the seventeen being The Purple One. The slogan for the trade in the 1930s was 'put your shop in Quality Street by putting Quality Street in your shop'. Heath Robinson and Mabel Lucie Atwell were among the artists commissioned to draw for Mackintosh, most famously for the Toffee Town advertisements. The purchase of Bellamy's and then Fox's brought liquorice allsorts and Fox's Glacier Mints respectively into the catalogues. Other products included Beehive Toffee and Creamy Rolls in the 1920s, Cresta in 1950 – Caramac in 1959 – Cracknel Bon-Bons, Toffo, Toffee Crisp, Golden Toffee Wafers, Munchies, the Weekend assortment in 1957 and Good News in 1960. Mackintosh was acquired by Rowntree's in 1969; Rowntree Mackintosh was then bought by Nestlé in 1988. The 1897 showcard illustrates how far the company, like others, went to associate themselves with the higher strata of Victorian society, and indeed with Victoria – as represented by her coat of arms.

CHAPTER 10

Maynard's, London
& Sheffield

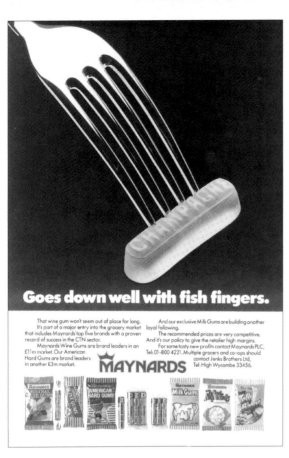

Goes down well with fish fingers.

That wine gum won't seem out of place for long. It's part of a major entry into the grocery market that includes Maynards top five brands with a proven record of success in the CTN sector.

Maynards Wine Gums are brand leaders in an £11m market. Our American Hard Gums are brand leaders in another £3m market.

And our exclusive Milk Gums are building another loyal following.

The recommended prices are very competitive. And it's our policy to give the retailer high margins.

For some tasty new profits contact Maynards PLC, Tel: 01-800 4221. Multiple grocers and co-ops should contact Jenks Brothers Ltd, Tel: High Wycombe 33456.

MAYNARDS

Wine Gums for a Methodist

Tom and Charles Riley Maynard began making sweets in 1880 in their kitchen in Stamford Hill, London. Next door, Charles's wife, Sarah Ann, looked after the sweet shop which sold their products. In 1896 the Maynard's sweet company was established. It was Charles Gordon Maynard who suggested to his Methodist and teetotal father that they make wine gums. Initially incandescent at the thought, Charles Riley eventually relented, comforted in the knowledge that the gums would contain no alcoholic wine. Maynard's Original Wine Gums were launched in 1909. By 1930 the company owned 250 shops, eighteen of which were bombed in the war (seventeen reopened) and a warehouse was built in York in 1937 followed by a new one in 1976. In 1959 there were 300 shops, the largest specialist confectionery chain in Europe. Maynard's merged with Barrett's in 1990 and in 1998 were bought by Cadbury who continue to manufacture their lines in Sheffield. The Week-End tin is from 1925. The card on page 41 showing the shop in High Holborn is franked 1904 and sent to Brussels.

CHAPTER 11

Needler's, Hull

Frederick Needler

Needler's was a significant force in the industry in the early twentieth century. Frederick Needler, a Methodist from Arnold, Skirlaugh near Hull, was working in a Hull tea and coffee warehouse at fourteen. He bought a small manufacturing confectionery business comprising two stoves, slabs, rollers and other basic plant with £100 of his mother's savings when he was eighteen and set up in Anne Street near Paragon Station in 1886. The company simply consisted of a sugar boiler and a boy called Watson, assisted by a delivery horse, with cart. The top photograph on page 43 is one of the earliest corporate pictures showing Spring Street around 1900. The wedding photograph is Frederick Needler's wedding on 7 September 1898. The 1906 Sculcoates Lane factory is on this page showing the Hull & Barnsley Railway in the distance; jar packing in 1910 is the subject of the other photograph.

Health Sweets and Rock

In 1900 he was employing ten female and twenty-three male workers producing a variety of lines: thirty-eight different boiled sweets, forty types of toffees, thirty-five health sweets, fourteen pralines and fifteen different labelled sticks of rock. The upper photograph shows the gas lit number 2 boiling room in 1910. The cooked sugars are formed into a rope before being made into sweets: humbugs are on the front table. A horse-drawn Needler van proceeds up Spring Bank in 1905 – note the telephone number, '90X', and the poster outside Coult's Newsagents announcing 'Japan's advance in Manchuria' during the 1904–1905 Russo–Japanese War.

Stollwerk

The company was also wholesaler for other firms, such as the German Quaker company Stollwerk, Cadbury's, Fry's, Craven's, Taverner's and Rowntree's (see Price List on page 50). This ended in 1912 when the product range was 576 lines of which 74 were chocolate. In 1906 a new five-storey chocolate plant was built in Lotus Avenue off Bournemouth Street to cater for this. Mr Lazenby was hired from Carsons of Bristol, a division of Packers. The sepia photograph shows a 1935 trade show display; despite what we like to think the jars, sadly, were not full of sweets – they were all face-packed with paper stuffed in the middle to support the sweets on the outside. The stunning colour picture is taken from the 1926 catalogue.

The Wilberforce Box

By 1920 turnover was £570,000, comprising 650 tons of chocolate and 1,500 tons of sweets, with a range now including Christmas boxes and Easter eggs. There were 1,700 employees, mostly women. In 1929 the catalogue featured twelve different assortment boxes and numerous chocolate bars. The boxes gloried in such names as Wilberforce, Minaret, Lido, Eldora, Carlton and Crown Derby. Kreema milk chocolate was advertised as being 'creamy! velvety! delicious!' A pre-1914 trade show is in the upper photograph with over 120 different boiled sweets in four different types of glass jars. The 1939 catalogue shows some innovative packaging for Christmas with attractive receptacles, practical and ornamental.

GALLEON FLOWER HOLDER

A wonderfully realistic antique galleon, beautifully made in Staffordshire semi-porcelain. Special holes for flowers. Large hole at the back for emptying and cleaning. 7½" high, 9" across.

Needler's

5'6

Containing ¼ lb. (2/- worth) County Chocolates.

"RIPPLE" WATER SET

What could be more natural than this smart Ripple design. Here is a gift for every day use at a truly wonderful price. Containing ½ lb. (3/- worth) County Chocolates.

6'6

Automation and Hump-Shunting

Sales were boosted when green sweet jars were replaced by clear glass. Air conditioning was installed in 1927 permitting all-weather packing; wrappers had been introduced in the early 1920s and wrapping was automated in 1928. Up to 1918 goods were shipped either by horse-drawn vans or crated and sent by rail. A fleet of vans was built up and by 1927 there were forty delivery vans, all smartly liveried in chocolate brown. The speed limit was 20 mph rising to 30 mph in 1930. Rail distribution was terminated in 1950 when British Rail introduced hump-shunting which resulted in unacceptable levels of jar breakages. The firm's exhibition vans were requisitioned in 1939 and never seen again. Exports for Foramaya Facatativa via Puerto Rico are depicted in the top photograph taken around 1922 and the 1939 catalogue in colour.

Glace Fruit Drops

Needler's innovative chemists perfected clear fruit drops – Glace Fruit Drops – in 1938, resulting in another lift in sales. They had the market more or less to themselves until 1965 before they were commercially challenged. In 1938 production moved away from chocolate although post-war demand for Glace Fruit Drops still exceeded supply until 1957. A good selection from 1926 with a very plush vanity box 'dainty fluted ribboned diamond shaped casket in blue, containing 1lb nett County Chocolates de Luxe'. The other wonderful photograph shows a Ford AT 5624 decorated for second prize in 1920.

49

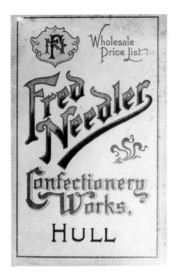

Cover of price list 1899.

FRED NEEDLER,

→ MANUFACTURING CONFECTIONER ←

Works—9 & 11, SPRING STREET, HULL.
Office—11, SPRING STREET, HULL.

Branch Establishment—
1, SOUTH PARADE, HILDERTHORPE,
BRIDLINGTON QUAY.

Agent for Fry's, Cadbury's, Rowntree's, Stollwerck's, Allen's,
Clarke, Nickolls & Coombe's Chocolates ; and Barratt & Co.'s,
Faulder's, Terry's, Craven's and other makers of First-class
Confectionery : Dealer in Snow Glasses, Glass Dishes,
Scales, and Shop Fittings, etc.

TERMS.

Carriage Paid on **25/-** worth of Goods and upwards, less 2½ per
cent, for cash on journey.

EMPTIES.—These should be returned as soon as possible, **Carriage
Paid**, and advised in detail. We allow in full for all cases, bottles,
&c., sent out by us, when received in good condition, but cannot
allow for others. We advise receipt of all empties on arrival, and
customers may then deduct the amount for which they have received
Credit Notes.

BREAKAGES.—When receiving Goods please sign for them **"not
examined,"** and if there are any breakages advise the Railway
Company at once. This allows us to make a claim on the carriers
in case of damage or shortage, or carriers will not recognise claim.

Cash to accompany Order. Credit Account opened by special arrange-
ment.

Prices are subject to market fluctuations.

Inside cover of 1899 price list.

Raymond Needler

Raymond Needler succeeded Percival Needler as Managing Director in 1970; he promptly bought London confectioners Batger, famous for their Jersey Toffees and Sainsbury own brand products. Dickson Orde of Farnham was acquired next. Chocolate production was finally ended in 1976 under pressure from the likes of Cadbury, Rowntree and Mars. The firm focused on sugar confectionery and toffees, laid off half of the 800 staff and returned a profit in 1977, the first for a number of years. The 1899 Price List is illustrated here – note the list of agencies, the dealership for shop fittings, and the Bridlington branch. The 1926 catalogue page shows twelve out of over 100 assortment boxes available.

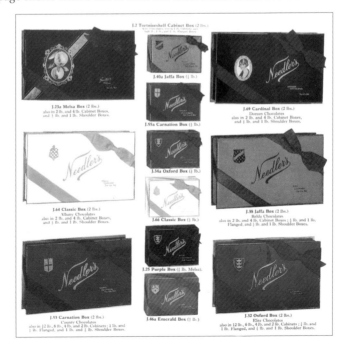

Needler Hall

Like George Cadbury and Joseph Rowntree, Frederick Needler was a non-conformist and a philanthropist. He was a Methodist Sunday school teacher for many years; he married another Sunday school teacher in 1898 after breaking off a previous engagement and going through a law suit for breach of promise. The company had a strong reputation for good industrial welfare: a profit sharing scheme was introduced as early as 1911, the pension scheme for men started in 1922 and there were excellent dining, social and sports facilities. Needler's renowned Musical Society was set up in 1925, performing occasionally on the BBC. Frederick was a close friend of Tom Ferens of Reckitt's (also a Methodist) who was involved in the founding of University College, now the University of Hull. Frederick Needler personally bought and then gifted Needler Hall in Cottingham to the College as a men's hall of residence. A Ford Model 18F is pictured here with 'period streamlined body' and below more practical and entertaining quality receptacles.

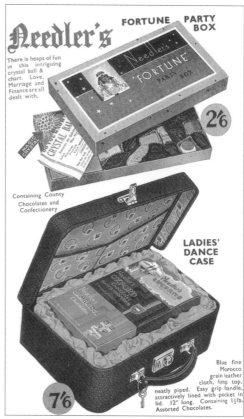

Needler's FORTUNE PARTY BOX

There is heaps of fun in this intriguing crystal ball & chart. Love, Marriage and Finance are all dealt with.

2'6

Containing County Chocolates and Confectionery

LADIES' DANCE CASE

Blue fine Morocco grain leather cloth, limp top, neatly piped. Easy grip handle, attractively lined with pocket in lid. 12" long. Containing 1½lb. Assorted Chocolates.

7'6

Black & White Colour Catalogues

Hillsdown holdings bought Needler's in 1986 along with Bluebird Toffee of Birmingham. Nora AS, Norway's biggest food group, bought the company in 1988, although sweets continued to be produced in Hull under the Needler brand name. The sepia photograph shows the Prince of Wales leaving the Bournemouth Street entrance after his visit in October 1926. The Christmas Boxes pictured here were typical of the fifty or so available; they were made and printed on site and the ribbons were hand tied after packing. Amazingly, all the catalogues were photographed in black and white and then skilfully coloured in by hand using water colours; these colour pictures were then converted into three colour separations and printed up in house.

CHOCOLAT AU LAIT
AUX AMANDES GRILLÉES

NESTLÉ

MILCHSCHOKOLADE MIT GEROSTETEN MANDELN

CHAPTER 12

Nestlé, Vevey & York

A BIT OF OLD YORK.

Half-pound
block

1'-

also in bars at
twopence each

The broadest wink
Jane ever wunk
Was when she grasped
Her Nestlé's chunk.

Farine Lactée Henri Nestlé Company
Henri Nestlé, a German, was born in
Frankfurt in 1814. In 1875, twenty-two
years after moving to Vevey on Lake
Geneva in 1843, the chemist started
making *farine lactée*, a baby food
(*Kindermehl*) made from Alpine milk
in powder form and ground cereal.
Henri Nestlé and Daniel Peter with
Jean-Jacques Kohler, his chocolate
manufacturing neighbours, then
went on to develop the first real milk
chocolate when the three businessmen
combined their products to produce
Chocolat au Lait Gala Peter – 'The
Original Milk Chocolate' – in 1874.
Henri opened a sales office in London
in 1883 for the Farine Lactée Henri
Nestlé Company and in 1901 its first
UK factory started production. The
pictures on page 53 show an early
wrapper in French and German for the
Swiss market; the 1905 comic postcard
depicts one of York's horse-drawn
trams passing Fishergate Postern
advertising Nestlé farinaceous milk
and Nixey's of Soho Square stove
cleaner. It conceals a controversial side
of York's transport history when the
horses of York Tramway Company's
were reputedly ill treated before
they were decommissioned in 1909;
the series of cards were intended to
scorn the company and its (human)
employees. The *Jane* advert appeared
in *Punch* in 1928.

'It's the Milky Bar Kid'
In 1905 Nestlé merged with the
Anglo–Swiss Condensed Milk
Company, established in 1866,
to form the Nestlé and Anglo-
Swiss Milk Company. High street
sales were boosted by Nestlé's
extensive use of the new vending
machines which were springing
up everywhere and which, in this
case, dispensed 1*d* chocolate bars.
In 1904 they formed an agreement
to import and sell Kohler & Cailler
products, thus strengthening their
position in the UK market. In 1913
chocolate production began at
Hayes. The white chocolate Milky
Bar was launched in 1937. It soon
gained a reputation for being
'good for children' on the basis
that it contained only cocoa butter,
sugar and milk, made entirely
from natural ingredients without
artificial colours or flavours. Nearly
half a pint of milk is poured into
every 100 grams of chocolate.

Rowntree Mackintosh

In 1988 Nestlé acquired Rowntree Mackintosh after a bid by Jacobs-Suchard for the York company was rejected. The year 2010 saw Nestlé celebrate the 75th anniversary of KitKat; the Nestlé UK website gives us the following amazing statistics: over 1 billion [KitKats] are eaten in the UK every year equal to 564 fingers every second; 17.6 billion fingers are eaten across the world every year; the largest single retail outlet for KitKat is Dubai Duty Free, which sells over 1 ton per day. Three million KitKats are made every day in York. The Jungly chocolate biscuit was made in Barcelona for the Spanish speaking markets.

Nuttall's

Curiously

STRONG MINTS

*Despite their diminutive nature,
one should not underestimate the
ability of these small peppermints to
refresh the palate.*

CHAPTER 13

Nuttall's, Doncaster

NUTTALL'S MINTOES REG°

A DELICIOUS COMBINATION OF
TREACLE BUTTER AND SUGAR
Be Sure You Say NUTTALL'S MINTOES
and avoid Imitations

Enjoy them while you play.

Nuttall's Mintoes
Harry Nuttall established the confectionery business in Doncaster. His son William succeeded him and opened a new factory in 1909 in Holmes Market employing 130 people. In 1912 Nuttall's Mintoes were launched; so successful and popular were they that production of other sweets like the Liquorice Lump was suspended to satisfy demand. Later the company was taken over by Callard & Bowser who continued to sell the sweets under the Nuttall's name. Like others in the confectionery business William Nuttall was a noted philanthropist, donating large sums of money to help the people of Doncaster, and on his death in 1934 he left £221,000.

CHAPTER 14

Rowntree's York

Rowntree US Exports, 1886

The Rowntree story starts with the tenacious, enterprising and Quaker Mary Tuke. In 1725, age thirty, Mary opened a grocery business first in Walmgate, then Castlegate, and, after a number of legal wrangles with York Merchant Adventurers Company, finally won the right to trade as a grocer in 1732. Her nephew William joined the firm in 1746 and inherited the business on Mary's death in 1752, now specialising in the sale of coffee, chicory and drinking chocolate. His son Henry came on board in 1785 and they began to sell tea and to manufacture cocoa and chocolate themselves. On this page we see Arthur Archer making an advertising display in the Tray Shop, photographed for the *Golden Jubilee Issue* of *CWM* in Spring 1952. The other marvellous picture in the Spring 1970 issue shows Alfred L. Wright of Wright & Rich, Druggists and Grocers of Boston, Massachusetts, around 1886 delivering Rowntree products.

Samuel Tuke

Henry's grandson, Samuel Tuke, was a good friend of fellow Quaker Joseph Rowntree I and was related to him through marriage; Joseph, too, ran a grocer's shop, in Pavement. Samuel's sons, meanwhile, were more interested in banking and teamed up with their relatives the Barclays; they had no interest in the York cocoa business. In July 1862 Joseph's son, Henry Isaac Rowntree (who had served his apprenticeship both at the family shop in Pavement and at Tuke's), bought the Tukes' business. The firm was small, with twelve staff and sales of about £3,000 – 10 per cent of Cadbury sales and 5 per cent of Fry sales at the time. The best performing brand was Tukes's Superior Cocoa, later to become Rowntree's Prize Medal Rock Cocoa. The colourful *Tots* trade advert dates from 1968.

61

DIFFERENT…

for her, AERO—the milk
chocolate that's different!

Joseph Rowntree II

Henry relocated the firm to an old foundry at Tanner's Moat
in 1864. However, the combination of Henry's preoccupation
with his Quaker activities, old technology and short run
manufacturing techniques stifled any real progress; in short, the
business was ailing. Help was at hand, though: in 1869 he was
joined by his brother, Joseph Rowntree II, and the firm
H. I. Rowntree & Co was established. Joseph injected much
needed business sense by focusing on the financial and sales
side, leaving manufacturing to Henry; in effect he probably
saved the 'hopelessly embarrassed' company from (a very un-
Quakerly) bankruptcy, bailing out a brother who 'knew next
to nothing of the business'. The 1951 *Aero* advertisement was
in *Illustrated* magazine. The famous Black Magic diary adverts
featured in *Reader's Digest.*

The Claude Gaget Effect

A sales call by Claude Gaget in 1879 had a major impact on Rowntree's. Gaget was working for Compagnie Française, Parisian confectioners, in London. The samples of gums and pastilles he presented that day eventually led to Rowntree's manufacture in 1881 (but only when the product was perfected and of the highest quality) of their famous Crystallized Gum Pastilles. An immediate success, sales of the pastilles galvanised the company and they expanded into nearby North Street. By 1885, 4 tons were being produced weekly. Staff too doubled to 200 in 1883 and sales more than doubled from 1880 (£44,000) to 1889 (£99,000); net profits increased five-fold from around £372 in 1879 to £1,649 in 1889. These sweets were of course the precursors of Rowntrees Fruit Gums and Fruit Pastilles. Violet Carson, aka Ena Sharples from *Coronation Street*, is photographed here for *Cocoa Works Magazine* with her box of Dairy Box.

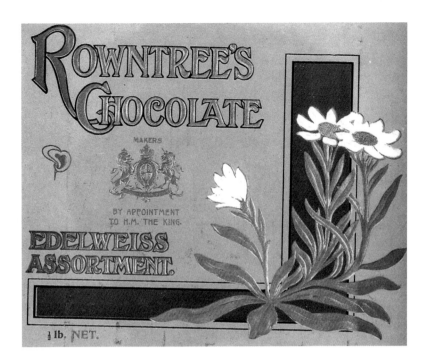

Haxby Road

This success also enabled Joseph to invest in new machinery in 1880, notably a van Houten press for the production in York of cocoa essence – Rowntree's Elect, 'more than a drink, a food' and made from top quality cocoa. Overall output remained low. Notwithstanding, Joseph bought a twenty acre site on Haxby Road in 1890 for a more efficient and ergonomic factory which would enable the firm to meet the anticipated growing demand for their products. The factory had its own railway line and halt and by 1898 all production was on the new site; the number of employees in 1884 was 182, by 1899 this had rocketed to 1613. The pictures on page 59 show the Haxby Road site in the 1940s and part of it today – up for sale for redevelopment. The comical pastilles image is on a small show card from the early 1900s, complete with moving legs on discs to represent the children running.

New Earswick

On the social welfare side, Joseph Rowntree emulated the Cadburys by establishing the Joseph Rowntree Trust and beginning the building of New Earswick, a new garden village, at the turn of the century. The objective was to provide the worker of even the most modest means with a new type of house that was clean, sanitary and efficient. Rowntree's deep concern for the welfare of his workers, his research findings and those of his son, Seebohm, into the plight of the urban poor, his Quaker beliefs, Cadbury's achievements at Bournville and the pioneering work on garden cities by Ebenezer Howard all combined to drive the establishment of New Earswick just minutes away from the Haxby Road factory. The upper advertisement was in *Picture Post* in 1950; the lower in *Reader's Digest* in the late 1950s.

Aero Takes Off

It was the appointment and rise of sales manager, marketing director and future chairman George Harris, a friend of Forrest Mars, which began to make a real difference. Harris' experience of American marketing methods, product development, branding and advertising eventually led to the change from a conservative, production led company to a market driven one ultimately resulting in the launch of KitKat, Black Magic, Aero, Dairy Box, Smarties and Polo in the 1930s. It was Aero, an aerated rather than a solid chocolate, which provided Rowntree's first real success, in 1935. Aero was originally to be called Airways to reflect the increase in jet travel in the 1930s; in the end it was branded Aero, a name originally registered with Cadbury but transferred over to Rowntree. Aero soon started to eat into the massively successful Cadbury Dairy Milk's market share. The wonderful advert on the upper left was drawn by Alan Mott, aged eight, and published in *Illustrated* in 1952.

A Journal in the Interest of the Empoyees of Rowntree & Co Ltd, York March 1902 saw the publication of the inaugural issue of the *Cocoa Works Magazine*, or *CWM*; the final issue was in May 1986. For eighty-four years it provided an intriguing and detailed record of life at Rowntree from the board to the shop floor. Subtitled *A Journal in the Interest of the Empoyees of Rowntree & Co Ltd, York*, its purpose was to keep everyone informed about what was going on at all levels. The showcards date from around 1925.

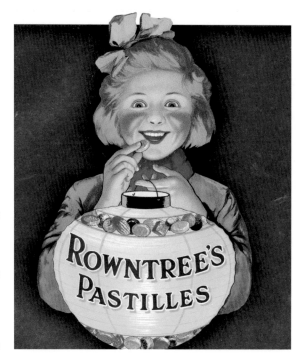

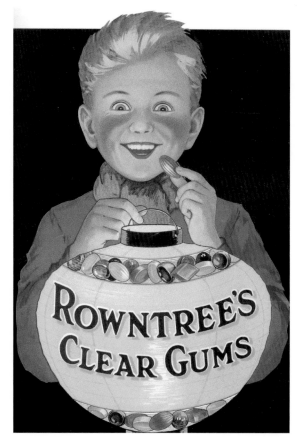

County Industries Ltd

In the Second World War chocolate companies, Mars for example, were either closed for the duration, transformed into completely different companies in support of the war effort – Rowntree's 'became' County Industries Ltd – or else they hosted other war manufacturers: Rowntree manufactured Oxford Marmalade on behalf of Frank Cooper Ltd. The brief for County Industries Ltd was mainly to produce shell and mine fuses in the Smarties block. The York Chocolates advertisement appeared in *Punch* in 1927, emphasising fashionable society of the day and the role chocolate always had, and still apparently has, in the wooing of women.

National Milk Cocoa, Ryvita and Household Milk

At Rowntree 300 clerks of the Royal Army Pay Corps moved in as did York firm Cooke, Troughton & Simms for the manufacture of optical instruments. Out of the Cream Department came National Milk Cocoa, Ryvita, Household Milk and dried egg. The Card Box Mill swapped production of fancy boxes for supplies for the RASC, Northern Command. Part of the Dining Block became a refuge for blitzed families, notably in the aftermath of the 1942 Baedecker Raid; a VAD hospital with 100 or so beds occupied the rest of the building. There was also a nursery to allow mothers of young children to come to work. At any one time sixty children could be accommodated; cots were made by the work's joiners and the orchard became the playground. Easter egg packers featured on the cover of the Spring 1970 edition of *CWM*.

Mackintosh

Rowntree merged with Mackintosh in 1969, so bringing such famous brands as Rolo, Toffee Crisp, Toffo, Weekend and Quality Street to the fold. Unusually targeted more at the male than the traditional female market, Yorkie was launched in 1976 to compete with Cadbury's Dairy Milk and to meet the demand for a chunkier alternative to the much thinner Dairy Milk bars. Yorkie was soon a major success with sales of 13,000 tons by 1978. KitKat, though, continued to dominate. In 1988 Rowntree Mackintosh was acquired by Nestlé. The After Eight advertisement was in the *Observer Magazine* in 1974.

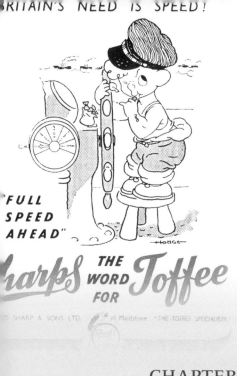

"FULL
SPEED
AHEAD"

CHAPTER 15

Sharp's, Maidstone & York

Sir Kreemy Knut

The Sharp's brand was launched in 1911 from their Kreemy Works factory in Maidstone; the company was headed by Edward Sharp, a Congregationalist. Sharp's best-selling line was Super-Kreem Toffee, from 'The Largest Manufacturers of Toffee in the World'. Royal Nougat was another important brand. Over the years they were taken over by Taverner's, Trebor Bassett and Monkhill and are now part of Tangerine Confectionery of York. The brand was relaunched in 2004 as Sharp's of York in a campaign which resurrected the same monocled, bowler-hatted toff, Sir Kreemy Knut who characterised Sharp's toffee from 1911. The character is much sought after today as a Royal Doulton figure. A knut is a dandy. The adverts on page 71 were published in *Punch* in the late 1940s. The skater on this page was featured in 1952 while Sir Kreemy Knut, quite appropriately, featured in the programme for the Royal Film Performance in 1954 attended by Her Majesty the Queen.

CHAPTER 16

Terry's, York

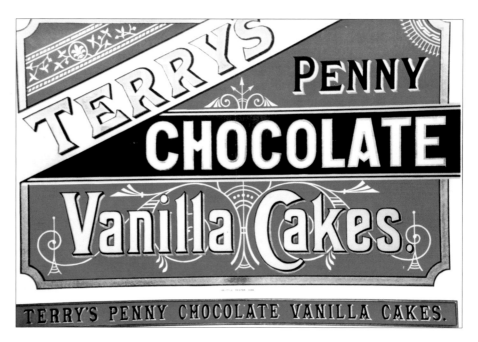

TERRY'S PENNY CHOCOLATE VANILLA CAKES.

Joseph Terry

Joseph Terry started making cocoa and chocolate in 1886 and had become the market leader of chocolate assortments by the end of the 1920s. Joseph came to York from nearby Pocklington to serve an apprenticeship in apothecary in Stonegate. An advertisement in the *York Courant* in 1813 tells us that he is established 'opposite the Castle, selling spices, pickling vinegar, essence of spruce, patent medicines and perfumery' – the usual stock in trade for an apothecary. The photographs on page 73 show a Betty & Taylor's van delivering to Betty's and parked outside the former Terry's restaurant in York's St Helen's Square, and the Terry's tower and famous clock today.

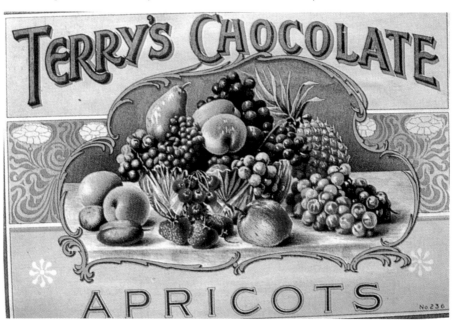

Terry & Berry

Later, he moved this chemist's shop to Walmgate. In 1823 he married Harriet Atkinson who was related to Robert Berry; he ran a small confectionery business with William Bayldon near Bootham Bar. Joseph then gave up apothecary and joined Berry in St Helen's Square. George Berry succeeded his father to form Terry & Berry but George left in 1826 leaving Joseph to develop the confectionery business. The 1885 showcard shows Terry's Clementhorpe factory and illustrates the preoccupation with French chocolate – at that time the chocolate makers to emulate. The Theobroma display card evokes the 1930s and promotes the chocolates in a book-type box. Theobroma was the Linnaean taxonomical name for the cacoa tree, and means 'food of the gods' in Greek.

'How Do You Flirt?'

Terry's wasted no time in going national; by 1840 their products were reaching seventy-five towns all over England. They included candied eringo, coltfoot rock, gum balls and lozenges made from squill, camphor and horehound. Apart from boiled sweets production included marmalade, marzipan, mushroom ketchup and calves' jelly. Conversation Lozenges, precursors of Love Hearts, with risqué slogans such as 'Can you polka?', 'I want a wife', 'Do you love me?' and 'How do you flirt?' were particularly popular. Chocolate production began in earnest around 1867 with thirteen products adding to the other 380 or so confectionery and parfait lines. Associating Terry's chocolates with the New World and the age of discovery is in the *Punch* advertisement of 1964.

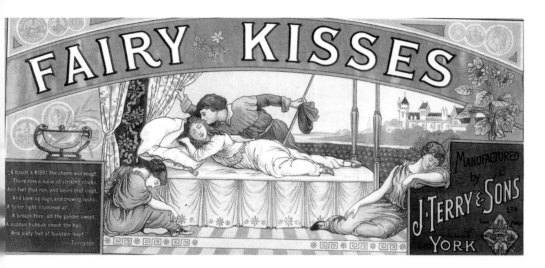

St Helen's Square

When he died in 1850 Joseph left the business to his son, Joseph Junior, then aged twenty-two. In 1864 Joseph leased a riverside factory at Clementhorpe on the River Ouse. St Helen's Square was retained and converted into a shop, ballroom and restaurant; you can still see the Terry name on the building's façade. Joseph Jnr died in 1898 and was succeeded by his sons Thomas Walker Leaper Terry and Frank Terry. The famous Neapolitans brand was launched in 1899. The Fairy Kisses box dates from 1885, as do the Lilliputian labels on this page and on the next.

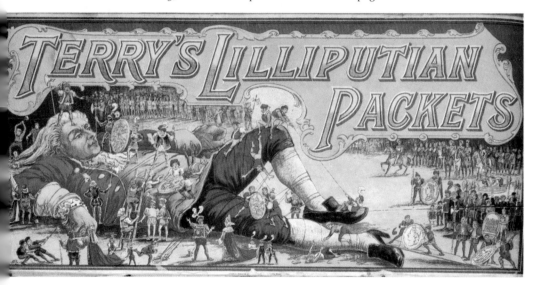

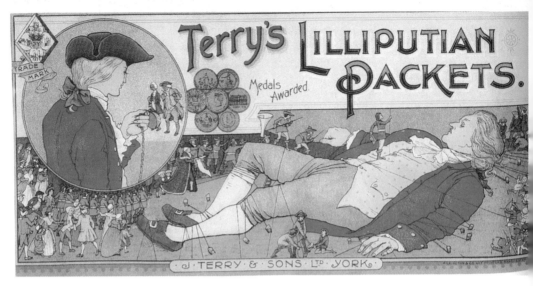

All Gold and Chocolate Orange

In 1926 the company moved again to the purpose-built Chocolate Works in Bishopthorpe Road. Between the years 1918 and 1938 revenues doubled as did tonnage sold rising from 2,332 tons in 1925 to 4,836; employees stood at 2,500 in 1937, 60 per cent of whom were women. These increases were due in part to the launch in 1932 of All Gold and Chocolate Orange. Up to the Second World War, Theatre Chocolates were available with their unique rustle-proof wrappers.

By an amazing act of metamorphosis Chocolate Orange started life as Chocolate Apple (phased out in 1954); one in ten Christmas stockings reputedly contained a Terry's Chocolate Orange at one time. The Forte Group bought Terry's in 1963; Forte already owned the Hammersmith based Fuller's confectioners and cake manufacturers. The then Lord Mayor, Mona Armitage, questioned whether Terry's had been fortified or Forte had been terrified. The company was taken over by Kraft in 2003; for the time being chocolate stayed in York with sugar confectionery concentrated in Bridgend. In 2004 Kraft made 6,000 redundancies across all of their operations. Terry's York closure was announced with the loss of 316 jobs.

CHAPTER 17

Henry Thorne & Co., Leeds

The World's Premier Toffee

Like others in the confectionery industry, Henry Thorne was a Quaker. His first shop which opened in Briggate around 1837 sold mustard and chicory but this quickly grew into one of the country's bigger confectionery companies. They embraced new technology, notably steam power, and pioneered the use of photography on their tins. By the 1960s Thorne's (their slogan was 'The World's Premier Toffee') was producing over two million pieces of confectionery a day. In 1971 the business moved into the premises of their sister company C. W. Mattock, confectioners and 'toffery' of Sowerby Bridge, and the factory, in Lady Lane, was closed and demolished. The seaside picture on the can pictured here is one of a splendid series by Mabel Lucie Atwell who also worked on Toffee Town for Mackintosh.

CHAPTER 18

Thornton's Sheffield

Chocolate Kabins

Joseph William Thornton left his job as a sales representative for the Don Confectionery Company in 1911 and opened his first Thornton's Chocolate Kabin shop on the corner of Norfolk Street and Howard Street in Sheffield. Products included Violet Cachous, Sweet-Lips, Phul-Nanas and Curiously Strong Mints. Chocolate production began in 1913 in the back room of their second shop on the Moor. Easter eggs and Thornton's Special Toffee were the main lines until the 1950s when the Continental Chocolates range was launched. In 1948 the company moved to Belper and in 1954, Walter Willen, a Swiss confectioner, joined and created Swiss Assortment – a range of handmade confectionery. The name had to be changed to Continental Assortment after complaints from the Swiss Embassy. Thornton's today turns over £215 million with 400 shops and cafés and around 200 franchises. They are the largest independent chocolate and confectionery company in the United Kingdom.

CHAPTER 19

Whitaker's, Skipton

Claire Whitaker

Whitaker's began as a grocery and drapery shop in Crosshills run by John and Rebecca Whitaker around 1889. Their daughter Ida, a trained baker, persuaded her father to specialise as a baker and confectioner. He did and produce was made in a room behind the shop, sold in the front while the family lived above. They moved in 1926 to the High Street, Skipton, and opened a restaurant above the shop. Claire, after whom the shop is today named, was the mother of John Whitaker, who is still chairman today and grandmother of William, the current managing director. Among their bestsellers are Mint Wafer, Mint Cremes and Mint Crisp made with an old family recipe; these are currently the world's best selling after dinner mint chocolates and are to be found in hotels (usually on your pillow), in restaurants, on airplanes and in supermarkets as own brands as well as in the usual sweet shops. In 1999 Chocolate Neapolitan was successfully launched: half a million of these are made every day out of an average daily production total of 1,500,000 chocolates. The pictures on page 83 show the shop in Skipton High Street and on this page we see workers enjoying a game of cricket during a break.

CHAPTER 20

Some Other Yorkshire Confectionery Companies

Barrett's, London and York

Founded in London in 1848, Barratt's became market leaders in the 'children's own-purchase' market, making an extensive range of 1d sweets including Sherbet Fountains and Black Jacks. They were taken over by Bassetts in 1966; their brands are now manufactured by Tangerine Confectionery. The Lip Sticks label dates from around 1935.

Bellamy's, Castleford

Joseph Bellamy first started manufacturing confectionery in Leeds but in 1900 moved to Castleford where sweets are 'spice' and liquorice is 'Spanish'. The factory in Queens Street was previously the Mountain Nail Works but was converted to a liquorice refinery and a sweet factory. Apart from liquorice allsorts they were famous for Mint Imperials and French Almonds. The business moved to Wheldale Mills on Wheldon Road and remained in the family until it was bought by Mackintosh in 1964.

They really are good

BELLAMY'S

LIQUORICE ALLSORTS
FRENCH ALMOND
POMFRET CAKES
MINT IMPERIALS
AND CHOCOLATE

JOSEPH BELLAMY & SONS LTD · CASTLEFORD · YORKS

R. S. Brownhill & Sons, Leeds

Made feculina, a flavoured flour used in making cakes of different flavours, butterscotch, peppermint rock, lozenges, fruit pastilles, Turkish delight and other sweets. They were active in the Wellington Works from the 1890s and described themselves as wholesale druggists, dry-salters and manufacturing confectioners. They also operated from Stand No. 10 at the Grocery Exchange, every Tuesday in the Corn Exchange, Leeds and became known as Brownhill-White Ltd, noted for their Crestona Butterscotch. See page 85.

Bellamy's
the name for super confectionery
Children's Favourites

Giant Assorted

YO-YO

Jelly Tools

Pomfret Cakes
Liquorice Allsorts
Jelly Babies
Mint Imperials
Torpedoes

mint oodles

Joseph Bellamy & Sons Limited
Wheldon Road Castleford Yorkshire WF 10 2JN

10

2

87

Callard & Bowser, London and York

Finchley was the original home of this firm established in 1837 by Daniel Callard and his brother in law, J. Bowser. Their speciality was Creamline Toffee. They bought William Nuttall of Doncaster and were themselves bought by Terry's of York in 1982. The posters date from the 1890s.

Don Confectionery Co., Sheffield

Somewhat unfairly, the Don Confectionery Co. is best remembered as the company which Joseph Thornton left in 1911 to set up on his own. Don Confectionery was established by Samuel Meggitt Johnson in 1878; Johnson was managing director of Bassett's but he needed somewhere for George Bassett's two sons to work, apparently, because he did not want them in the Bassett's business. The company was bought by Bassett's in 1933.

PARKINSON'S

Lion Confectionery, Cleckheaton

Lion have been synonymous with Midget Gems since they opened their factory in Westgate in 1902. They are still in Cleckheaton turning out thousands of tonnes of gum-based products every year and still using a steam boiler from 1926 called Helen. Lion are now owned by Tangerine.

Parkinson's, Doncaster

Doncaster Butterscotch is first recorded in 1848 and was sold by three rival Doncaster firms: S. Parkinson & Sons (possibly the inventors), Henry Hall, and Booth's. Parkinson Ltd was established by Samuel Parkinson, confectioner, grocer and tea dealer, in High Street Doncaster in the early nineteenth century. Their butterscotch was promoted as Royal Doncaster Butterscotch or The Queen's Sweetmeat, and reputedly 'the best emollient for the chest in the winter season'. It was to become one of Doncaster's most famous exports and a highlight of the St Leger race week. In 1956 they employed 600 or so people, mostly women. In 1961 the company was acquired by the Holland's Confectionery Group. The business ceased production in 1977. Today, Parkinson's Doncaster Butterscotch Company makes all of its butterscotch to the original recipe in Doncaster. The poster, from 1925, assures us that the tins, like the children, are 'too full for words'.

Radiance, Doncaster

Lines included Devon Cream Toffee, Hazelnut Toffee, Extra Devon Cream, Creme-De-Menthe, Radiance Assortment, Riviera Assortment, Chocolate-Coated Toffees, Brazil Toffee. They were closed by 1943.

Riley's, Halifax

Fred and J. H. Riley set up their confectionery business in Halifax in 1907. Their premier line was Toffee Rolls, available in seven flavours including fig, rum and butter, date and liquorice. Initially, the factory was in the family home but saw a move to Hopwood Lane and the Kingston Toffee Mills in 1911, famous for the Riley name on the 120-foot-high chimney picked out in seven foot white glazed letters. On J. H. Riley's death in 1953 Nuttall's bought the company; later, Callard & Bowser, Smith Kendon, Terry's of York and finally Kraft all bought Riley's. Ella Riley wrote down the recipe 'just in case' and it lay dormant in her cookery book for many years until 2008 when it was found by Freya Sykes, her granddaughter. Freya bought the rights to Toffee Rolls and now produces them under the name Ella Riley Ltd, selling them at Ella Riley's Toffee and Traditional Sweet Shops in Horbury Bridge and Holmfirth. The superb railway tin on page 91 is also a Riley tin.

J. Roggall & Sons, Leeds

Manufacturers of toffees, liquorice and nougat. The original factory was in Rockingham Street, where the Merrion Centre is now. By 1930 they were in Spark Street. It was here that they were granted permission to employ on two day-shifts, 'women of 18 years of age and over in attending automatic wrapping machines and weighing up and packing in the Toffee Department'. By the 1950s they were in Seacroft.

A. L. Simpkin & Co. Ltd, Sheffield

The company was founded in 1921 by Albert Leslie Simpkin. They were the first manufacturers of travel sweets. The strategy was to make high quality glucose confections using natural flavours and colours and to sell them through the chemists' shops, a niche market which avoided competition with the large confectionery manufacturers. By 1924 he had 80 per cent coverage of the UK with 12,000 accounts, soon employing 180 workers. The range was extended from bulk barley sugar drops in jars to include powdered sweets in 8 oz reasonably airtight travel tins. They were called travel tins because they contained barley sugar drops which can alleviate the symptoms of travel sickness. Today, domestic sales are still mainly through chemist and health food outlets.

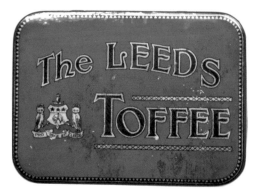

Slade & Bullock, Dewsbury

Ben Bullock was a Burnley miner who moved to Dewsbury in 1868 and set up stall selling boiled sweets in Dewsbury and Heckmondwike markets. In 1876 he established his own company and introduced what was reputedly the first example of lettered rock. The *Dewsbury Reporter* takes up the story in 1976: 'Ben turned out his first batch of lettered rock with the words 'Whoa Emma' inside them as a tribute to a popular song of the day. The Whoa Emma rock sold like magic at West Riding markets but bigger things were yet to come. The discovery of a paper which could cover the sticks of rock and yet be removed easily coincided with Ben's decision to take a fortnight's holiday ... [in] Blackpool. Shortly afterwards a few hundredweight of Blackpool lettered rock was sent to the resort and the novelty so caught the public fancy that the Dewsbury firm was inundated with orders from seaside resorts all over Britain. [Ben Bullock's] fame spread abroad and demands for lettered rock arrived from all over the world, with exports going to such places as Malta, the Sudan, India and Australia.' In 1930 H. W. Bywaters, D.Sc, Director of Slade & Bullock Ltd, and former Chief Chemist at J. S. Fry & Sons, authored *Modern Methods of Cocoa and Chocolate Manufacture*, which was published by Churchill. See the Slade & Bullock tin on page 90. The illustrations show the Leeds Toffee tin from about 1910 manufactured by Pickles & Co, 6 Boar Lane, Leeds, established 1874, containing chocolate and sweets for dessert – not Thorne's, and possibly a short-lived competitor – and one from Royd's of Drighlington. Other manufacturers include Swan Confectionery Works Hull; Toffee Smiths, Halifax; Evans & Priestman, Hull; Goldsborough Toffees Ltd, Brewerton Street, Knaresborough – wound up in 1929 – see page 89; and RK Confectionery, Hull – see page 34.

CHAPTER 21

Confectionery in Twenty-First-Century Yorkshire

Confectionary in the High Street

After many years of what can only be described as commercial complacency, Yorkshire, and York in particular, seems to have woken up to the realisation that it is the country's confectionery capital. The pictures on page 93 illustrate the increasing presence and popularity of confectionery in the high street. Sweets, quite rightly, have not escaped the current vogue for artisan production and this development brings us full circle and back to the nineteenth-century days when sweets and chocolate were made on a piecemeal basis, sometimes in the manufacturer's own kitchen. York has its fair share of these modern-day chocolatiers. There is a branch of the chain, Hotel Chocolat, in Coney Street which, like their nineteenth-century forebears, trades on the cachet that association with all things French gave to chocolate; Monk Bar Chocolatiers of York opened in Goodramgate in 1999 with a second branch in Shambles opening in 2002. Choc-affair in Naburn have been producing quality chocolate since 2008.

York Cocoa House

York Cocoa House in Blake Street was the city's first dedicated chocolate house since the Tuke's establishment in the 1820s. Opened in late 2011 it produces, and serves, chocolate and cocoa on the premises; it is run by Sophie Jewett who also owns Little Pretty Things, established in 2009 to provide 'a home for true chocolate lovers!' The core business is regular chocolate-making parties, talks and classes, chocolate-tasting sessions and workshops illuminating York's chocolate industry heritage. The pictures show Annie Gray, food historian, at the opening of the Cocoa House and chocolate making at a Little Pretty Things workshop.

The Sweet History of York

A new Nestlé UK state-of-the-art archive at the Haxby Road site was launched in 2011. Many of the items, which includes 37,000 photographs and over 100 hours of film, will be exhibited at various places and at various events in the city. 2012 looks set to be an important year for chocolate in York. A £2 million project, The Sweet History of York, a visitor attraction celebrating the city's confectionery heritage, opens in King's Square; this is York's second confectionery visitor attraction – see page 19. It will allow visitors to see at first hand the story of York's confectionery industry, past, present and future; there will be a strong emphasis on hands-on activities, anecdotes and memories from former employees of Rowntree, Terry and Craven, and visitors can have a try at making their own chocolate. A four day Chocolate Festival begins in April with a series of events celebrating the city's confectionery heritage, 'as York becomes transformed into a Chocolate City and the industry, chocolate lovers, artisan chocolatiers, museums and attractions share a piece of York's chocolate history'. The pictures show The Sweet History of York under construction and Easter eggs in the window of Little Betty's Café in Stonegate.